The Art of Landscape Quilting

Nancy Zieman and Natalie Sewell

©2007 Nancy Zieman and Natalie Sewell

Published by

krause publications

An Imprint of F+W Publications

700 East State Street • Iola, WI 54990-0001
715-445-2214 • 888-457-2873
www.krausebooks.com

Our toll-free number to place an order or obtain a free catalog is (800) 258-0929.

The following registered trademark terms and companies appear in this publication: Fiskars®, Gingher, Quick Fix, Skydes™, HeatnBond Lite®, Warm & Natural®, Warm Company™.

Library of Congress Catalog Number: 2006934238
ISBN 13-digit: 978-0-89689-314-6

Designed by Heidi Bittner-Zastrow
Edited by Tracy L. Conradt
Photography by: Dale Hall

Printed in China

About This Book

Since the publication of our first book, *Landscape Quilts* (Oxmoor House, 2001), our passion for making landscapes from fabric has grown. So, inevitably, has our list of techniques we wish we had included the first time around. Realizing, to our amazement, that since the appearance of *Landscape Quilts* we have created more than 60 new pieces, we decided to write this book to incorporate our new ideas into our approach to landscape quilting.

Our first book, *Landscape Quilts*, is a "how-to" book. Landscape quilting was still in its infancy and readers wanted not only detailed instructions on all of our techniques but an introduction to the concept. We knew as we wrote it that our methods of using raw edges, "messy" cutting techniques, laundry markers and paper glue sticks as our tools had broken many traditional quilting rules. Because all of those methods still hold true for us today, *Landscape Quilts* remains a popular and helpful book.

But today, landscape quilting is an established technique. According to the latest "Quilting in America" survey, 33% of all quilters say landscape quilting is their favorite quilt design. We no longer have to introduce quilters to the concept. We know from talking with quilters everywhere that people want to see as many landscape quilts as possible and learn to make them.

For that reason we've designed *The Art of Landscape Quilting* as a personal journey through our quilt collections. Because most land-scape quilts are horizontal, we've turned the format sideways (the book is 10" by 7" rather than 8" by 11") and depicted not only the quilts, the fabrics and the tools we used, but the steps and stages we went through to create them. Sometimes those stages aren't attractive and sometimes they're wrong turns but we show them to you anyway.

Apart from Chapter One on how to get started and Chapter Seven on how to finish your quilt, the text is personal. We each describe our own landscape quilt, what we hoped for when we began, what the journey was like and why we think we succeeded or failed. We know from our teaching experiences that you will learn just as much from our wrong steps as our right ones.

The best way to use this book is to read it through from start to finish, then mark the quilts that use techniques you want for your own landscapes. Although we depict several quilts step-by-step, most of the time we focus on the challenging aspects of each scene, such as how to shade an oak tree, how to create distant foliage, how to paint the lines of sidings on a front porch. Our hope is that you will use our tips and tricks to create effects in your own landscape scenes inspired by photos you love... and that you will have a happy landscape quilt journey of your own.

—Natalie and Nancy

Table of Contents

About this Book

Chapter 1
How to Begin

Welcome to the art of landscape quilting. We think you may be surprised to learn how simple these nature scenes are to make. You will not need templates, patterns or complex tools. You don't need to know how to draw. Scissors, some fabric markers, a few glue sticks and a small collection of cotton fabrics will get you started.

The leaves, trees and shrubbery that cover our landscape quilts are simply motifs from our landscape fabrics which we cut out, glue and machine appliqué to background fabrics. We enhance the motifs with fabric paint or pastels, and then machine quilt and bind the piece. This technique allows almost as much spontaneity as painting does. And the final result can be as unique as you are.

Out On A Limb
by Nancy Zieman (47" x 40")

Photos for Inspiration

Artists who use paint, pastels or pencil can bring their tools directly to the scene that inspires them and create on site. Fiber artists cannot. We have to depend on photographs not only for our inspiration but also for assessing scale, texture, hue, and depth in our scenes. Even when the photo is only a jumping off point for a landscape quilt, it plays a very important role.

The most important characteristic of any photo you consider as your inspiration for a landscape quilt is that you love it. You find yourself looking at it repeatedly and intensely. The site it depicts means a lot to you. You rush to your fabric stash (or local fabric store) to find matches for the elements in it —the bark, the leaves, the water, the rocks, etc. You put it in a special place and come back to it time after time. Since you will be spending untold hours recreating it in fabric, you need to care about it.

The second most important characteristic of your photo choice is that it be fairly good. It does not have to be of professional quality but its hues should be intense enough to show you where the light is coming from. Its details should be vivid. Its perspective should be one you can reproduce easily. Remember that you will be interpreting the photo and translating it into art, not copying it. If it has elements or structures you don't want or need, leave them out. Change the type of trees at your will; reduce or enlarge the foliage. You are the artist.

The final consideration should be who took the photo. Let's say that one of your landscape quilts wins a prize at a quilt show or gets noticed by your local newspaper and you are asked to provide not only a photo of it but of the scene that inspired it. Photographs are protected by copyright laws. If your landscape quilt is inspired by a professional photo from a book, calendar, magazine, or print, you must get permission to reprint it in any form. Permission from publishers or professional photographers can be hard to come by and sometimes involves a long, legal process.

For that reason, the safest path is to use either your own photos or ones taken by friends, family, or local photographers who are often only too happy to give you permission to reprint their work. We have learned from experience to bring our cameras along on any outing that may lead to a landscape quilt inspiration. Given our passion for landscape quilting, that means we carry our cameras everywhere.

Some Landscape Quilts and the Photos That Inspired Them

The Red Canoe by Natalie Sewell (45" x 41")

The photo that inspired this quilt appeared on the cover of the April 2004 issue of *Wisconsin Trails* magazine. I was in the middle of designing a wooded scene when it arrived. The cover took my breath away. The red canoe was the perfect foreground for my new quilt. Within hours, I had a lakeshore, a red canoe, and, with the help of fabric paint, a reflection. Photographer Carol Miller's shot was so in harmony with my woods that I didn't have to change a branch or a blade of grass. I simply added the new foreground to my existing woods. In this case I used the inspirational photo as a close-up of my foreground, while the wooded background that comprised the rest of the quilt came from my imagination.

Photo by Carol Miller
for Wisconsin Trails Magazine.
(Photo used with permission.)

Almost Autumn by Natalie Sewell (56" x 37")

A simple snapshot that I took myself one fall day inspired Almost Autumn. I took many liberties with the photo. Notice that I avoided the ground altogether and completely ignored botanical accuracy. But the photo helped to shape my foliage and trees, especially in the distant background.

Black-eyed Susans Along the Barn by Natalie Sewell (44" x 29")

I found this charming photo by Alaine Johnson at a local art show. Alaine had superimposed the flowers onto the barn wall. I loved the sparseness of the scene and the "end of summer" feel of the old blooms which I recreated from bits of hand-dyed fabric enhanced with acrylic paint. The barn wall proved to be the easiest part, given the wonderful commercial wood fabric available today at fabric stores. However, the rusty hardware was challenging. Notice that my scene has many more blossoms than the photograph depicts. When I reached the same number of blossoms that the photo depicted, my fabric scene seemed too bare. I always feel free to abandon my photo inspiration once I have begun to design my scene.

Photo by Alaine Johnson.
(Photo used with permission.)

The Red Barn by Nancy Zieman (44" x 31")

I took this photo in 1974 as part of a photography class assignment. Never did I realize that many years later it would serve as an inspiration for a quilt. You'll learn why I chose maple leaves to frame the scene rather than pine boughs on page 80.

Choosing Fabrics

The variety of fabrics available to quilters today is almost infinite. Deciding which fabrics to use for your landscape is an important part of what will make your scene uniquely yours. There are very few wrong choices. What follows are a few general tips to help guide you.

Background Fabric

Your background fabric can set the mood of your scene and make your creative experience much more manageable if you choose wisely. The only rule of thumb when deciding what fabric to use for the background of your scene is to avoid solids, which stop the eye. Look for a mottled texture that is neither too busy nor too quiet. Squint at it to see if it suggests the kind of foliage you want to depict. If you choose carefully, you can save yourself countless hours of cutting and gluing pieces to cover the parts of your background fabric that don't work.

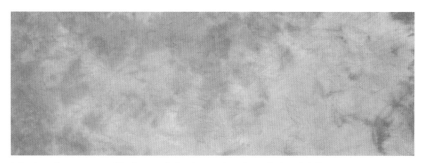

Notice the areas of light and dark on this hand-dyed fabric.

Hand-dyed Fabric

Hand-dyed fabric makes a great background choice because of its irregular images. The very process of making hand-dyed fabric ensures that there will be no repeats of patterns in your scene. Its mottled textures are wonderful for shaded shrubbery and suggest distant wooded scenes that lend great depth to your landscape. Until recently hand-dyes were hard to find. Now they are readily available online if you can't find them at your local quilt store. In addition, many current quilt books teach easy methods of dyeing your own fabric, if that interests you. Although hand-dyes are somewhat more expensive than commercial fabric, they are well worth the extra money for the unique character they lend your quilt.

Hand-dyed fabrics are ideal background choices and are available in almost every hue.

Commercial Fabric

Commercially produced fabric, especially batiks, can make ideal backgrounds for landscape scenes as long as you avoid those with geometric designs and too many shapes and hues. They are available at almost every fabric store these days and, like the ones depicted on page 12, can be as subtle and effective as a hand-dyed fabric.

Here are some batik fabrics available by the yard in most quilt shops.

Making the Choice

Look at the difference the background fabric can make in the photos below. Nancy's quilt, *Blooming Fence*, began with a very dark and vibrant hand-dyed background fabric. However, she wanted a subtle, soft-hued effect. The dark fabric made the fence, foliage and blossoms look faded and flat. By changing to a paler, more subtle background, she was able to create the mood she wanted.

Nancy wasn't happy with the mood of the quilt until she changed the background fabric.

Fabrics for Tree Bark, Wooden Structures and Fences

Wood fabrics for trees, structures and fences come in a variety of shades and textures. You will need several if you are planning a scene that has depth. To achieve a sense of distance, the trees (or fences and structures) need to diminish in tone and color as you move toward the back of the scene. The foreground trees, for example, may be black or deep brown, while the trees in the middle ground are dark gray or light brown. The most distant tree (or fence) may be just a pale gray or neutral color. The textures in the fabric can also help with creating distance. Intense foreground texture should fade as you move back in the scene—until it almost disappears. For these effects, you will need a wide variety of wood fabrics.

Fabrics for Ground Cover

The key to choosing effective ground cover fabric is scale. The smaller the better as long as there is a variety of hues. Much of your ground cover fabric will be interrupted later by foreground elements such as tree trunks, flowers or grasses, so don't worry if it seems dull. The eye needs a resting place between focal points in the foreground and distance—ground cover provides that.

Fabrics for Leaves

For many landscape scenes, leaves are the dominant feature. They need to be interesting and varied. Even in summer scenes, a variety of leaf colors ranging from purple to blue-green to chartreuse add vitality to your quilt. Touches of yellow and white leaf fabrics lend a sun-kissed touch. Don't worry too much about botanical accuracy. Pay more attention to scale. Distant leaves need to be paler and smaller while foreground leaves are more intense in hue and considerably larger. Repeating sections of leaf fabrics several times in your scene decreases "busyness" and seems more natural.

Fabrics for Flowers

Flowers are often one of the focal points of a landscape scene. Use them sparingly. If you fill your design with too many, your scene may look more like wallpaper than a garden. A rule of thumb for deciding how many flowers you can use is approximately one for every thirty leaves. We have learned from experience that more is not better when it comes to depicting flowers.

When choosing floral fabric, pay no attention to the background color or leaves in the design. You will probably be cutting away the background fabric and finding the leaves so sparse as to be useless. Pay attention only to the blossoms: are they the right color for your garden? Are some of the flowers turned to different angles so that they look credible in your scene? Take care with the scale of your flowers. If your fabric contains only large ones, perhaps you can cut them a bit smaller for more distant views.

Three Simple Techniques

Once you've chosen a photo inspiration and selected your fabric, you'll be ready to start designing.
To complete your design, you will need to use three simple techniques.

Messy Cutting

Messy cutting is ideal for distant shrubs, ground cover, foliage, and leaves. It requires you to cut "as poorly as possible," creating uneven jagged edges and asymmetrical bumps and lumps of fabric so that foliage looks natural. Any scissors will do but the easiest to use is a small clipper-like tool made by Fiskars.

Fussy Cutting

Fussy cutting is the best technique for foreground flowers, leaves, plants and grasses. It's simply the process of cutting carefully along the object's edge, following the lines of the printed motif. Since such work can be tedious and slow, we recommend sitting down to do it while listening to music or watching TV. The best tool for fussy cutting is a very sharp, small embroidery scissors. We like Gingher's embroidery shears, but any will do.

Gluing

Glue is the best medium for attaching all of your cut motifs to the background fabric. And the best type of glue for this purpose is a paper glue stick. The glue stick spreads thinly and evenly and will hold for weeks or even months—until you are satisfied with your design and have a chance to stitch down your motifs at the sewing machine.

Don't glue tentatively. Lay your motif down on a piece of batting and apply glue over the entire outer edge of each motif. If you glue too lightly, your pieces will fly around as soon as you move your design from the wall to your machine.

There are many fusible webs on the market for attaching one fabric to another, but they tend to stiffen the quilt top and reduce the loft you achieve when you machine quilt. Because you will be using many tiny pieces of many different fabrics, fusing each one of them could be tedious.

The glue stick allows for great spontaneity. Because it's designed for paper, you can pull off and move the motif you've glued whenever you change your mind about where it should go.

Don't worry. Paper glue will not gum up your sewing machine.

Design Wall Options

Creating your landscape scene on a vertical surface allows you to step back and see what you've done, what you need to do next, and what doesn't work. A vertical surface allows you to view your scene at different times of the day in different light, day after day.

If you have the room and the skills, by all means make a permanent design wall, as big as the space allows. We have used pine—permanently mounted and then covered with thick batting and then a white flannel sheet that stretches to 112" by 65". But you may want a much simpler design wall, especially if you are new to landscape quilting. Corkboard, foam core, or even insulation board can make a very adequate vertical surface, either mounted on a wall or even propped up against a wall. If you cover your surface with batting and then flannel, you'll find that pieces of fabric stick in place while you step back to see if you like where they are.

Since your finished quilt will hang on a wall, it's wise to design vertically as well.

Painting on Fabric

No matter how big a landscape fabric stash you have, you will still have shading, shadows, sunlight, and dappled light to create in your scene that nothing short of paint can achieve. The more landscape quilts we make, the more we rely on paints to enhance our fabric quilts.

The only requirement of the paint you use is that it be permanent. Even though you will not be sending your landscape quilt through the washing machine, you will be blocking it with steam and the paint, like the dyes in the fabric itself, must be waterproof. It's best to test any paint on a scrap that you attempt to wash before you apply it to your scene.

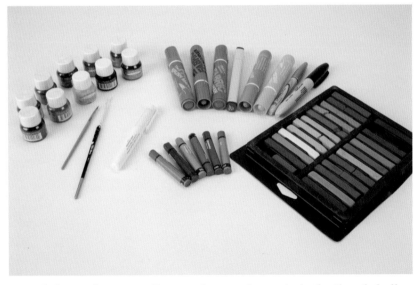

From left to right are acrylics, markers, and pastels, both oil and chalk.

Markers

Permanent ink markers are the easiest paints for beginners to use. Available in art and office supply stores, they come in a wide assortment of colors, need no mixing, and dry quickly on fabric. Because they change the color of a motif without concealing its shape, they are ideal for landscape quilts. Notice in the top photo how yellow and gold markers change white daisies to yellow with streaks of gold in their petals with no loss of detail. In the lower photo, a gray marker and a silver marker change a snow-white picket fence into a more credible one. Note also how the silver metallic pen is creating shadows that give dimension to the fence.

It's easy to change the colors of flowers with markers.

Shading adds depth to a picket fence.

Acrylics

Acrylics are water-based paints that dry very quickly. When applied thickly, they have the advantage of over painting, thus allowing fiber artists to change a hue permanently and quickly. Unlike fabric markers, they completely hide the original motif rather than simply change its color. Because they can be mixed to exactly the color you want, they offer a distinct advantage.

Pastels

Both oil pastels and chalk pastels are very effective on fabric and we use them often. They come in a wide range of vivid as well as subtle colors, which can be blended right on the fabric. Rub the pastels with your fingers or sponges to create soft effects like the petals of flowers. For grass-like effects use sharp tools like pencils or sticks. Spray the pastels with fixatives which set them permanently onto your landscape quilt.

Chapter 2
Simple Landscape Scenes

Simple scenes can be elegant and moving, not just easy to make. We created the scenes featured in this chapter because we were inspired by their loveliness, not because we needed easy quilts for our readers. But when we planned this book, it made good sense to place them here, near the beginning. Their easy construction makes them a perfect starting place for those of you new to landscape quilting. At the same time, the techniques we've used to complete them are the same ones we've used in our most intricate pieces. For that reason, we hope, even experienced landscape quilters will learn new tips.

In the Tree Tops *by Natalie Sewell (54" x 20")*

In the Tree Tops is a simple quilt to construct for several reasons. First, it depicts the mid-line of a group of birch trees which means there is no ground cover to create. Second, it's a close-up view which means fewer tree trunks, branches and leaves. Third, I used only three fabrics in the entire quilt.

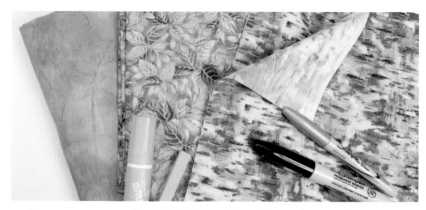

The secret to making this interesting design lies in the use of a gorgeous piece of hand-dyed fabric for the background and some painting tricks. A multi-hued hand-dye, its unusual size and coloration dictated the design. Its yellow and green hues suggested summer. Some mottled grey fabric for trees, mid-sized green leaves and a few fabric paints, were all I needed to complete the scene.

I hung the long strip of my background fabric on my design wall and studied it before I started the design.

Since birch tree trunks come in a variety of hues from white to dark gray, I used both the darker front and lighter back of mottled gray fabric for the bark. This scene has a total of 13 fabric tree trunks, some fat, some skinny. (Nine of the skinny trees were hand-drawn onto the background after all the fabric cutouts were in place.) The two largest tree trunks measure 3" across. The thinnest are less than half an inch. If you create this design, feel free to use these numbers only as a rough guide, since your background fabric may be a different size and your tree and leaf fabric may have a very different scale.

I cut the tree trunks several inches taller than my background fabric and placed them onto the background fabric as shown. Notice that the trees are not upright like telephone poles but slightly tilted both to the right and to the left. Note also that they tend to be slightly narrower at the top than at the bottom.

When I was satisfied with the shape and number of trees I had placed, I began the gluing process. (For tips on gluing, see page 17.) I waited to shade my tree trunks with fabric paint until I had added all my leaves because they covered a large portion of each tree trunk.

If your leaf fabric is brilliant with a variety of hues that you love, you can skip this step. But if it's like mine, a little boring and flat, you can wake it up with fabric paint. As depicted in the photo, I used orange and yellow permanent markers to color the fabric before I fussy cut it into leaves. Painting the fabric before cutting saves a lot of time because you can do it with broad strokes of your marking pen.

Once you've painted and cut out your leaves, you are ready to place them onto the trees and branches. Of course, nature creates a thousand more leaves for every one that an artist creates, but the viewer's eye tends to fill in the scene for you. If you include too many leaves, your scene will become busy and labored.

The key in leaf placement is to clump them unevenly. The temptation to place them equidistant from each other is hard to resist, and I fight it with every landscape quilt I make. Make sure some leaves cover the trunks and branches and others seem to run off the edge of the background fabric to convey a sense of lushness.

Since birch trees have dramatic horizontal markings, they are easy and satisfying to paint. Make sure your horizontal lines curve a bit to depict the roundness of the trunk.

My favorite tools for painting birch trees are permanent black and gray or silver marking pens, some sharp and pointed, others brush tipped for bolder markings. Don't forget to add the blotches of black that characterize birches.

To shade your trees, first decide where the light in your scene is coming from. In my quilt, it's coming from the left, so I have darkened the right side of every tree and branch. Black marking pens are perfect for shading.

Use a sharp black marker to draw branches on your trees. Then, with a sharp gray or silver marker, draw another line alongside your black line, making it thicker as you approach the tree trunk. Your branch then will appear shaded.

This technique for drawing branches works equally well for drawing distant trees. Draw one black line, then a gray line along its side. The further away your tree is, the thinner your lines will be.

October *by Natalie Sewell (54" x 20")*

October was inspired by *In the Tree Tops*. I liked the long horizontal shape of *In the Tree Tops* so much that I created a fall version. To change seasons I merely changed the fabrics.

Notice the rusty and olive green hues of the background fabric. It's a lovely fall fabric but it lacked light as well as contrast. I found a yellow/gold fabric, messy cut out irregular globs from it and placed them randomly on the too dark background fabric before gluing the tree trunks in place.

To enhance the texture of the bark on the brown trees, I not only painted the bark with silver and black markers, just as I did in *In the Tree Tops*, I also added slivers of a blue wood fabric, then painted the blue edges with black to blend them into the brown bark. Note these three stages of bark painting in the photo above.

Wolf River Woods
by Nancy Zieman (41" x 34")

I designed this quilt, at the request of my mother, as a tribute to my father, Ralph Luedtke, long active in the governing affairs of Wolf River Township—a small farming community in Wisconsin where I grew up. It now hangs in his honor in the town hall.

You might have thought that I would have designed a quilt with a river. Yet the hundred acres of woods on our farm is what's dear to my heart and embedded in my mind. Hence, I didn't need an inspirational photo to do the designing.

The hand-dyed background fabric sets the mood for the scene—a sunny autumn day. The leaf and tree fabric choices seem to echo the colors playing across the canvas.

Three brown trees, one fat, two skinny, are the first elements in the quilt.

I added texture to the three trees by cutting strips of the remaining two bark fabrics and gluing them to the tree trunks. One of the fabrics had a splendid knothole which I cut out and glued to the fattest tree. After deciding that the light came from the left, I shaded all three trees on the right with a black marking pen.

Next, I added dark branches to all three trees by cutting skinny strips of my darkest fabric.

I began the slow but satisfying process of adding leaves, carefully cut from the large leaf fabric depicted in the photo on page 29.

After adding many more leaves (mostly red but a few green) I messy cut the two ground cover fabrics, using both their right and wrong sides. To enhance the fall mood, I "diced" up a few of the red and gold leaves with my scissors and sprinkled them on the ground cover. Notice how few leaves it takes to convey a wooded scene in fabric compared with the thousands a photograph would depict.

The design process continues after adding borders, pages 135-136. A few leaves and branches in the border lend drama to this design.

Tree Trunks in the Moonlight *by Natalie Sewell (31" x 41")*

As soon as I saw this lovely photograph by Kathryn Lederhause at a local art fair, I knew I soon would be struggling to recreate the dramatic play of light on tree bark in my next landscape quilt. I simplified the background detail by eliminating it. Instead I used a hand-dyed navy fabric which turned day into evening. Then I added a mere hint of brush and ground cover with a small-scaled green fabric. I used oil pastels to darken the top and bottom of the tree foliage and used white and yellow pastels to lighten the bark. Once the bark was lightened, I added dark lines with a sharp black marker to create the ridges that oak trees have.

Photo by Kathryn Lederhause. Kathryn took this shot at the Redwood National Forest in California on a fall day in September 1988. She says she "always looks for the play of the light on the land." (Photo used with permission.)

The Old Red Bud *by Natalie Sewell (57" x 20")*

The Old Red Bud is as much about a gorgeous green, metallic hand-dyed fabric that I couldn't bear to cover up as about a tree. Both the background and the tree fabric are hand-dyed Skydyes, created by Mickey Lawler (see Resources, page 142) and both feature metallic fabric paint. I added some silver and black fabric paint of my own in the sinuous tree branches. A thin black line—then a fat silver line—created the two-toned effect.

This simple quilt posed some serious design questions. Every time I added more blossoms and leaves I lost the starkness of the old tree. Finally I took almost all of them off and called it quits. But I still have them in a small plastic bag in case I change my mind again. One of the wonderful aspects of raw-edged appliqué is that I could put all the leaves and blossoms back onto the tree and no-one would notice I had changed a thing.

Winter Sunrise *by Natalie Sewell (41" x 48")*

The tree in this quilt literally grew in the making. I thought I was finished with my design in the photo, so I quilted, bordered, and bound it. Then I hung it on my wall. The tree was simply too small for the overwhelming sky. I took down the quilt, thickened the trunk and added several hundred more leaves, some protruding into the border. Then I hung it back on the wall.

Note how small the tree is in the early version.

Photo by Brent Schellinger. Brent described his photo's composition as a study of thirds—a third ground cover, a third solid sky and the top third streaked with gold. Brent's favorite subject is rural Wisconsin. (Photo used with permission.)

The pink and gold hand-dyed background fabric dominates this scene. Notice that the snow fabric is not pure white, but mottled shades of gray, with many darker textural lines. The leaves on the tree are tiny brown clusters—which made for many tedious hours of cutting. No wonder I tried to quit too soon.

Notice the grasses in the photo. I first made jagged cuts on a grass fabric, then glued them to the background snow fabric, then wove them into the scene by covering the grass fabric's edges with a silver marker. Hiding the raw edges of a cutout motif with fabric paint gives the landscape scene a sense of flow.

January In My Backyard
by Nancy Zieman (43" x 32")

One day, after a big snowfall, I grabbed my camera and took a photo of the blanket of white covering my backyard. Days later, when I held the print in my hand (see photo below), I couldn't help but notice the dramatic shadows cast by the trees. Instantly I knew the photo would become a landscape quilt.

I created the shadows by cutting simple slivers of mottled gray fabric and, with a gray marking pen, intensified them here and there. My snow fabric has blue and taupe shapes as well as light gray.

Moonlit Birches *by Nancy Zieman (35" x 44")*

My inspiration for this scene came from gazing outside in the wee hours of the morning to find the full moon casting brilliant shadows on the snow-covered ground. I was amazed to see that the trees had a pink hue! Months later, remembering that scene, I couldn't resist adding pink to my tree bark and to a few tenacious leaves as well.

I created the shadows with two shades of gray mottled fabric which I highlighted with fabric markers. Initially I eye-balled the placement of the shadows but they looked all wrong. Although I rarely use a ruler in the design process, I relied on one here for angling them correctly.

I love the way new snow clings to the crooks of the branches. I cut little triangles from my snow fabric and added them to my trees.

Birches in Snow by Natalie Sewell (40" x 49")

I created *Birches in Snow* with only two fabrics, the tree fabric used on both the right and the wrong sides, and an off-white background fabric. The design is simple and took only a few hours. However, the embroidery and quilting took weeks and weeks.

Before I layered the quilt, I machine-embroidered all the branches and the distant shrubs. I used silver metallic thread on many of the branches to create an icy effect. After I layered the scene, I quilted the top half—the sky—with small stipples, and the bottom half—the snow-covered ground—with short horizontal lines, leaving small puffy sections unquilted so that they protruded like tufts of snow. Then I used gray and silver markers to accentuate shadows on the snow, and black markers to shade the birch trees and make birch bark notches.

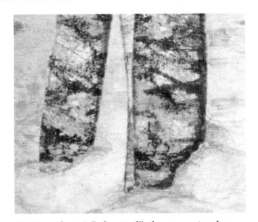

Notice that I "planted" the trees in the snow by cutting the bottoms of the trunks on an irregular slant.

January
by Natalie Sewell and Nancy Zieman (46" x 38")

January is one of the first quilts we made together and like so many of our winter quilts, it was easy to design. Snow cover hides so many details that even a novice quilter can achieve elegance quickly.

Our inspiration was a newspaper photo taken during a heavy snowstorm. As the trees receded in the distance they became fainter and fainter. A quick search through the fabric stash landed us three shades of gray.

The background is a piece of gray pointillist fabric that fortunately has little flecks that resemble snowflakes. We were lucky to find it. But any gray ombré fabric will work for a scene like this one.

Natalie sketched the little brown man on the walk with trepidation. She usually doesn't do human figures, but thought, "If he's walking away from us, how hard can he be?" She drew the figure on a piece of handdyed brown fabric, accented the coat and shoes with a dark marker, added a dark red scarf, and thought, "He looks just like my husband."

Chapter 3
Expanding the Scene

As you move beyond simple scenes and begin to tackle more complex landscapes that feature a myriad of foliage, ground cover, trees, water and sky, you'll be faced with many questions. Where do I start my scene? How much detail do I include? What should my focal point be? How do I choose fabrics that will help me create the mood I want?

Rather than answer these questions abstractly, one by one, we've selected 18 of our most challenging landscape quilts to explore with you. With several designs, we take you step by step through the process we undertook. With many others, we focus exclusively on the special challenge an aspect of the design posed for us. As we discuss all the challenges we faced and the solutions we found in the making of these pieces, we hope to give you a much clearer sense of how to tackle complex scenes of your own.

On My Path
by Natalie Sewell (49" x 38")

On My Path by Natalie Sewell
(49" x 38")

On My Path is one of those wooded scenes that come from memory rather than from a photograph. I've seen this scene a hundred times by the side of the roads we've taken to northern Wisconsin and the Upper Peninsula of Michigan. The time of year is early fall; the leaves are turning but the grass is still green in spots and everywhere are blotches of gold and red.

When I began this design, I pictured only a stand of trees. But, as often happens with landscape designs, the quilt developed a mind of its own and, in this case, it added a path.

Because my scene encompasses a wide area with many trees and shrubs, I knew I needed to choose fabrics with small-scale leaves. As you see in the photo above, the foliage fabrics have tiny motifs, except for the green leaves which I placed in the foreground. Notice that all the small leaf fabrics have a similar pattern—an impressionistic dot pattern rather than realistic tiny leaves. An important key to fabric choice is that the fabrics have a similar degree of realism.

For the background fabric I chose a navy hand-dye with rays of light—not because I wanted an evening scene, but because I needed a bold contrast for the rust and gold foliage. The two tree fabrics—light gray and charcoal black—became heavily painted and shaded once my design was complete.

Painters have the luxury of moving from foreground to background and forward again as they work. Landscape quilters need to start in the most distant background if they want to avoid constantly having to squeeze bits of fabric under previously glued pieces. For that reason I always start at the back of the scene.

I messy cut the top edge of the green grass-like fabric and covered the bottom edge with the darker of the two brown ground cover fabrics. I then messy cut my third fabric, the lighter ground cover, and let it extend to the bottom of the quilt.

Next I cut several thin, dark tree trunks and glued them on half way up the length of the quilt so they would appear to be growing in the most distant ground cover. I tilted them somewhat and curved their trunks slightly. As the trees came towards the foreground, I cut them fatter and taller and placed them lower on the background fabric.

Then I messy cut foliage from all three leaf fabrics. By clustering them somewhat—that is, the green foliage on the right side, the dark brown and rust in the middle, the bright orange and yellow leaves on the left side—I could begin to see the design emerge. I could see where the middle ground and foreground tree trunks should go and what I still needed to add.

At this point, it's important to step back from the design wall and decide if you are on the right track. Many times, I've come to this point and realized that my background fabric is just too busy, or that my leaf pattern is too large, too small, too pale, or too realistic. Making fabric changes at this point is so much easier than it will be later on.

Once I'm satisfied with the distant and middle ground of a scene I can focus on the foreground. In this quilt, that means the birch trees and the ground cover grasses. I cut six thin white birch tree trunks, glued them onto the scene and curved their trunks. Then I shaded them with a black fabric marker and made horizontal birch marks up and down the trunks. I added grasses to the ground cover, as well as some larger leaved plants which I painted red.

But, when I stepped back from the design wall I was disappointed. Nothing was happening in the scene. The foreground seemed to have little to do with the middle and background. The scene lacked depth and the eye of the viewer was stopped by the row of birch trees.

Frustrated, I pulled off a clump of birch trees—the three on the right side—applied a fresh coat of glue on their backsides and then placed them closer to the right edge.

I decided to create a path through my woods. I cut a large triangle from a piece of brown and beige batik that had blotches that resembled shadows. Then I messy cut the sides of the path, which created the illusion of shrubs and weeds. As it disappeared down a hill in the distance, I made it curve a little to add interest. Notice that it ends slightly before

it reaches the vanishing point. I drew horizontal lines on the path to differentiate it from the surrounding brush and made the foreground lines thicker and darker than the distant ones. Now the scene had depth and a focal point.

Rarely does a scene emerge intact from my mind to the design wall. I struggle with revisions on almost every landscape quilt I make, until I'm satisfied.

Here's a close-up view of the path.

Splash of Color
by Natalie Sewell and Nancy Zieman
(48" x 49")

The quilt, *Splash of Color*, began life with the name *Quiet Woods*. Our goal when we first created this scene was to make a truly calm and serene wooded quilt. As you can see from the fabrics in the photo below, except for the red leaves, all four leaf fabrics, as well as the background fabric, are shades of green.

We lived with our serene green scene for almost two years, passing it pleasantly back and forth from house to house without exchanging a word to each other about how we felt about it. But somehow we never got around to hanging it in shows. And then one day, one of us said to the other, "It would look very nice with some red leaves in the foreground."

Seven red-leafed branches made all the difference. Two of the upper branches extend into the borders on each side. One of the thicker branches begins in the left border. The entire revision took just a couple of hours.

Rural Route 1 by Natalie Sewell (37" x 24")

Rural Route 1 is a small quilt on a small subject. I've always been charmed by country mailboxes and I couldn't stop photographing them until I finally made a quilt about them. The photo depicts the mailbox for our cabin in the Upper Peninsula, as well as those of our neighbors. I've seen many more picturesque mailboxes than these, but they aren't ours.

I struggled with scale in the making of this simple quilt. I started with huge mailboxes, thinking they would encompass half the scene rather than the tiny fraction of space they ended up taking. But then, their importance became distorted. I started over three times until I found a mailbox size that was the right scale for my foliage. The template and the cut-out mailbox in the photo illustrate the scale I used. Note the silver marker in the photo which I used to create shadows on the boxes.

Notice, too, how dry and hot the road in the photo looks. It can get hot and dry up there in summer. One of the beauties of art is that it lets you shape reality in pleasing ways. I added more trees, more foliage, and a bit more shade. The grasses along the side of the road were challenging. I realized that it's easier to find lush foliage flowers in fabric than dry weeds and grass. I had to make my own. Oil pastels rubbed thickly onto the fabric and then scratched with pins and a fork did the job.

The Prairie by Nancy Zieman (44" x 32")

I've always loved coneflowers. The challenge I set for myself in this quilt was to create a meadow of coneflowers that seemed to extend for acres. To achieve depth, I had to reduce the size of the flowers in the distance and expand the ones in the foreground until they invaded the lower border.

I couldn't find a fabric with coneflowers, let alone one that had varying sizes of them. So I had to improvise. The tulip print in the above photo had exactly the right coloring for coneflowers. I cut out the tulips, cut them in half, then fringed the petals with a sharp scissors, and darkened their centers with a black permanent marker. The tulips had become coneflowers. As I worked towards the back of the scene, I cut each coneflower smaller and smaller until they virtually disappeared.

I often pin my quilt top back on my design wall after putting on the borders to see if extending the flowers or foliage into the border will help the design. In this quilt, the extension added great depth.

Spring In the Marsh by Nancy Zieman (51" x 25")

Because I lived for so many years near the Horicon National Wildlife Refuge, a 21,000 acre marsh, marsh scenes are imprinted in my mind. I thought I didn't need a photo for inspiration. In retrospect, I could have used one. No matter how familiar a landscape scene may be, the scale, color and shadows in an actual photo would have saved me time and frustration.

The four steps illustrate how I combined small clusters of four and five different fabrics to create each clump of marsh grass.

Notice how all the fabrics in shades of brown, green and gold work together to create these marsh grasses.

Here's a close-up view of the marsh grasses.

Birches by Natalie Sewell (77" x 50")

One October day, on my way up north to teach a workshop, I drove past a huge stand of birches. The bare tree trunks seemed to reach to infinity. I wondered if I could ever cut enough fabric trees to depict the impact of that scene in a quilt.

I was so impressed with the extent of the birch stand that I cut the biggest piece of background fabric I had ever used—77" wide by 50" deep. Then I began cutting birch trees. By the time I finished gluing them onto my background fabric, I had more than 60 distant trees as well as a handful of big ones that I placed in the foreground. Until I marked and shaded every single one of them, I wasn't sure I had a quilt worth saving.

As you can see in the photo, the markings had to be bold and dramatic. I worked my way through three large black permanent fabric markers before I was done with the scene.

The next challenge was to create effective ground cover. To evoke a sense of great depth I had to change the scale of my fabric dramatically from the lower left corner to the upper right side. The key was finding the large red leaves for the foreground and the tiny dot pattern of red, green and gold in the distance. And once the border was in place, I exaggerated the foreground by adding more big leaves.

The Old Woods by Natalie Sewell
(47" x 38")

Somewhere in my mind is a perfect woods. The trees stand in harmonious relationship to each other and the ground cover is lush with ferns, wildflowers and grasses. When I couldn't find a photo of this scene, I made the quilt anyway.

The trees are so old they have deep knotholes. I found a textured blue fabric that worked beautifully when I cut it into ovals and then made large black dots in the middle of them. Scattered in between the old dark trees are slender white ones, leaning ever so slightly and offering a perfect contrast to the dark gnarled trees.

The wildflowers, pink and white, are scattered about the ground cover. Just like the trees, the wildflowers are of an undetermined species. Such is the nature of a perfect woods.

Spring in Bloom by Natalie Sewell
(48" x 42")

Spring in Bloom is my second attempt at recreating the glory of redbud in a spring landscape quilt. I had learned an important lesson from my mistakes in the first spring quilt. The first spring scene had been cluttered with infinite detail: tiny leaves, tiny ferns, tiny blossoms, tiny trillium, and no focus for the viewer's eye.

This time I used a hand-dyed fabric for my background instead of a busy print. I moved the redbud trees further back on the background fabric so I could let the two-toned pink blossoms become clouds that drew the eye towards the back of the scene. I left out most of the individual leaves for the other trees; the few that remained were implied rather than detailed by a soft, gently spotted green fabric.

The issue of how many details to include preoccupies all artists, not just fiber artists. It's tempting for all new artists to be much too literal. But it's especially tempting for landscape quilters who work not with paints but with bits of already printed fabric. The key principle I try to remember is that I am creating impressions, not accurate reproductions. I've learned that a good "squint" of my eyes on a photograph will blur many of its details, and allow me to see the basic shapes in the scene. That blurred scene is the one I want to capture.

Ted's Quilt by Nancy Zieman (39" x 53")

When my oldest son, Ted, was in high school, he found a photo of tree trunks as they might look if you were lying on the ground. "You can do this scene," he said to me. I was delighted that he thought I could. And so I did. The quilt became a gift to him when he graduated from high school.

The trees in the photo are black and brown. However, I had the urge to make them teal blue, with hints of purple in the ground cover. Once I departed from the photo I felt exhilarated. As I cut out chartreuse and mauve leaves, I stopped referring to the photo altogether. I realized I would not be intimidated by a photo again.

Mt. Rainier on a Clear Day *by Nancy Zieman*
(34" by 41")

I'd traveled to the Seattle area many times but had never seen Mt. Rainier, thanks to one rainy day after another. Finally, on my tenth visit, there it was. The "mountain was out," as they say in the Pacific Northwest. I couldn't believe that something so huge and magnificent could have been so completely hidden from view.

To create the mountain, I used two batiks—a white one with blue blotches and a darker brown one with light tan areas. With the darker batik, I cut the shape of a large mountain. Then I cut curved areas of snow from the lighter batik and placed them randomly on the dark mountain. The light batik's blue blotches formed effective snow peaks and looked perfectly shaded.

Jerusalem by Natalie Sewell (68" x 55")

Jerusalem was inspired by a trip to Israel a few years ago to visit my sister. The time of year was March. Although I had been to Israel several times before, never had I seen the meadows in bloom as they were this time. The contrast between the ancient olive trees and the abundant new poppies seemed to symbolize the ancient city itself with all of its new outgrowth.

Unlike most of my quilts, which undergo extensive revisions and additions, this one came into being seemingly on its own. My goal with this quilt was to focus on the trunk of the olive tree, to convey its age and texture. I used at least eight different fabrics to create the trunk, as

This photo—especially the ancient olive tree—inspired Jerusalem.

well as fabric paint to connect the images and intensify the light and shadows. I was either truly inspired or very lucky as I got it on the first try.

Cutting the olive tree leaves from a very dense leaf fabric was tedious beyond belief and I did this, as I often do, sitting down watching a movie.

The poppies in this scene were made from at least seven floral fabrics. As you can see in the top right photo, many of them were neither the shape nor the color of poppies, but they were the right scale. I simply painted their petals red, darkened their centers with a black marking pen, and cut them in the shape of poppies, big ones for the foreground, and smaller for the distant view.

Out On A Limb by Nancy Zieman (47" x 40")

I enjoy creating the look of wood. When I saw a dramatic branch in a winter photo, I knew the scene was for me. I searched and searched for the perfect bark fabric but couldn't find it. The dilemma was solved when I came across an old rayon scarf—in particular, the wrong side of the scarf. Needless to say, that scarf is now tree bark.

The inspirational photo was a winter scene, but it was too stark for me. I changed the time of year to spring and the branch to a flowering crab. Adding blossoms and apple green leaves provided a warm contrast to the dramatic branch.

I ignored botanical accuracy and combined blossoms and leaves from different fabrics to achieve the look I wanted. A simple shading along the lower edges of the branches made them appear three-dimensional.

I cut distant tree trunks from a batik fabric, and gave them dimension with a few strokes of my marking pen. To create depth in the scene, I messy cut leaves from a small-scale leaf fabric and placed my leaves and painted trees behind the tree branch in the foreground.

By extending the branch and the foliage into the border, I was able to intensify the drama of the scene.

The First Day of Summer by Nancy Zieman (36" x 56")

The lush greenery found in the early days of a Midwestern summer is eye candy to me. I love the contrast of the white birches against the multi-hued green background.

I used approximately 20 different green fabric prints in this quilt—all scales and shades of light and dark leaves. It's not necessary to buy yards and yards of each fabric. Many small cuts of ½-yard pieces will give you plenty of design options.

This photo is a mini-lesson on creating a simple birch or aspen tree. Use both sides of a mottled fabric of light gray. Shade the tree with black and silver markers, add characteristic lines and dark blotches to the trunk, and cut slivers of black or very dark fabric to create thin branches.

Peak Color by Nancy Zieman
(46" x 32")

When I see the first hint of yellow or red in the foliage of maple trees, I know that Nature's color palette is about to make a dramatic change. There are three to four days a year when fall color is in its prime. *Peak Color* commemorates that brief but glorious period.

I shaded the larger trees with slashes of white marker as well as black and silver to intensify the brightness of the birch bark.

Chapter 4
Adding Structural Elements

Adding structural elements brings nature home to us and makes the landscape personal. Once you've learned to make trees and flowers, you'll want to customize them with landmarks you recognize, such as fences, gates, sheds, houses, gazebos. Adding structural elements dictates the type of trees and foliage you need, the season of the year, and even the weather. Suddenly you are faced with finding the right color of "paint" for your parents' barn, or the right shape of pickets for your neighbor's fence.

Structural elements require you to deal with perspective—that troublesome concept that gives depth and dimension to art. Building structural elements with fabric can be especially challenging. Flowers and leaves abound in fabric stores, but building materials, like concrete, wood, bricks and metals are a little harder to find. And even when you find them, it's difficult to make them fade in the distance, or get darker in recessed planes.

For that reason, we've organized the 13 quilts we feature in this chapter in order of difficulty, starting with the easiest. As we describe the challenges we faced with structure, we'll also explain how we tackled the landscape around the structures, and how we struggled in each quilt to create the illusion of depth. We are the first to admit that, at times, we didn't succeed. But we hope you benefit from our failures as well as our successes.

Fence Post by Nancy Zieman (41" x 34")

Fence Post by Nancy Zieman (41" x 34")

Creating a realistic fence out of fabric is just one artistic step beyond creating a tree. The post in this scene is constructed just like the trees in *Wolf River Woods* (see pages 28-30). I combined multiple bark fabrics and then added highlights with fabric pens to the make the post look realistic.

My inspiration for this quilt was a photo of a rail fence covered with clematis vines. I ignored everything in the snapshot except for one fence post and supplied my own hydrangea blooms from other floral fabrics. I often pick and choose elements from several photographs, and then improvise the rest of the scene.

Notice the right hand border in the finished quilt. To dramatize the rail in the foreground, I extended it into the border, making it just a bit wider so that it appeared closer. I did the same thing with the post in the bottom border. To create the sense that the rail was disappearing into the distance I decreased its size on the left and deliberately cut it off before the border.

I used three bark fabrics and a scrap of black for the fence post. I was careful to select contrasting shades (from light to dark). It's amazing how little color a scene needs to look natural. Use a few too many flowers and the scene looks artificial. The most impressive fabric in the quilt is the large leaf print. It's velveteen!

I started with the fence structure, gluing the vertical and horizontal post and rail shapes which I cut from the darkest bark fabric onto the hand-dyed background fabric. Notice that I tilted the post slightly to enhance the perspective. I then cut small sections of the light bark fabric to glue over the rail section to define the shape of the fence. Adding a small dark sliver of fabric for the rail opening in the post is what turned this "wood" into a rail fence.

Unmended Fences by Natalie Sewell
(44" x 49")

I've always loved old gardens—the ones where ivy and mosses invade the flower beds and move into the walls and fences; where one flower runs into another and no one fixes the fence for fear of interrupting the vines that grow on it. This is such a fence.

A picket fence that stretches across the width of a scene rather than receding into the distance is the simplest of structures to depict. But even this simple structure has dimension and requires perspective. The rail that supports the pickets is recessed and darker. I colored it with brown pastels. The pickets themselves, old, warped and hanging loose, show surfaces that need shading. I did that with dark gray markers. However, the real challenge in the scene turned out to be the light and dark shadows that play across the foliage between the pickets.

I've made garden scenes with picket fences before. Bright with blooms and lush foliage, they've all been neat and tidy. To make this one old and messy, I focused on the light in the scene. Dense shade implies large old trees and shrubs. By making the bottom left side very dark and gradually increasing the light towards the upper right, I achieved the dense look I wanted.

Notice the contrast between these two photos on the left. The top photo shows the bottom left corner of the quilt. To create the intense shade, I lifted the pickets and placed a dark hand-dyed fabric beneath them. Then I attacked the wood pickets with dark brown and black markers. I chose dark fabric leaves and added dark green acrylics to shade sections of the leaves. I also created leaf shadows on the pickets themselves with gray and black pastels.

The upper right hand corner was easier to create. I had used a hand-dyed background fabric with mottled light and dark sections and was careful to save a light section for this corner. I also chose white blossoms and light green fabrics which I dotted with white pastels, then covered the white with yellow pastels.

My progress while designing this quilt was not smooth. Sometimes sections became too dark and I had to start over. The transition from dark to light needed to be gradual and I at first made it too abrupt. At times my mistakes became virtues — in several spots, I lifted off glued-on leaves to find the unshaded areas beneath them were just what I needed.

Lots of fussy cutting and fabric painting went into this scene.

Natalie's Window by Nancy Zieman (46" x 31")

In the early days of our "quilting dates," Natalie and I worked on the same quilt. Recently, we've changed our approach. Now when we get together we each work on our own quilt, while freely sharing advice. *Natalie's Window* is just such a quilt. Without Natalie's help, this design would not have happened. Hence, it is affectionately named after her.

I used this fabric for both the blossoms and the leaves. Because the flowers did not match the leaf size, I had to cut them smaller.

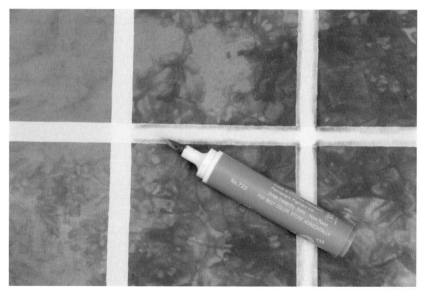

To keep the panes of the window as straight as possible, I used a fusible web instead of glue to hold the narrow strips in place. A thick line with a gray fabric marker along each side of the windowpane created the depth I needed.

The foliage is lush—a variety of fussy-cut leaves and small blooms. To give the scene depth, I overlapped the fabric cutouts and let them peek out behind each other.

Front Porch *by Nancy Zieman (40" by 45")*

For many summers our family spent long weekends at Mackinaw Island in the straits between Upper and Lower Michigan. I was always drawn to the neat and sometimes brightly painted wood-sided houses with lush window boxes. I couldn't resist taking a photo of the front porch of one of these houses for my next landscape quilt.

The photo of this front porch inspired my design.

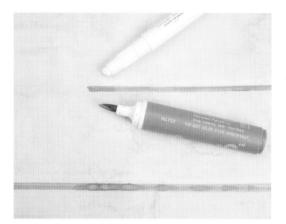

I struggled with how to create the wood siding. My solution was to draw parallel dark and light lines 3½" inches apart with a white-out pen and a gray marker. Of course, I used a ruler as well.

I needed geranium leaves but couldn't find them. Instead, I used a fabric that featured lily pads and cut them down to the right scale. I found a fabric with geranium blossoms but they were too small so I grouped flower clusters together until they were the right size for the scene. Then I added a "kiss" of sunlight to each one by whiting out a small section and then highlighting the white area with a brighter red marker.

Three Pots of Pansies *by Natalie Sewell (46" x 33")*

This simple quilt was a joy to make—it offered a respite between more challenging pieces. I had found some irresistible pansy fabric and I had spring fever. The pot fabric came from a commercial marbleized design, which when turned wrong side up, looked remarkably like red clay. Until Nancy came to quilt with me one day, it lacked depth. She suggested adding the shadows of the pots and that did it. Another landscape quilter's eye works wonders, we've discovered.

Aunt Alma's Window Box
by Nancy Zieman
(34" by 34")

This was my first window box quilt. You'll notice many fabric similarities between this quilt and my more recent design, *Front Porch*, on page 76. I chose to have the frame of the window also serve as the frame of the quilt.

This quilt hangs on a wall in my mom's family room. She tells me that guests often do a double take, wondering why she has a window box inside her home.

The Red Barn
by Nancy Zieman
(44" x 31")

When I shot this photo of my dad's barn through the branches of a pine tree in 1974, it was to fulfill an assignment to take a "framed" scene for a college photography class. The pine boughs served as the frame. Fast forward 30 plus years and this photo became the inspiration for a quilt. My quilted scene closely follows the structural details of the barn, but loosely interprets the "framing" portion. I replaced the pine boughs with maple leaves, which are not only brighter but easier to make.

I had this design in mind for many years, but couldn't begin until I found the right hand-dyed red fabric for the barn. The silo and sky fabrics were also important choices; I chose batiks.

This photo, taken at a very early stage, shows the structures without shading and painting. As you can see, fabric paints and markers help to give this design depth and perspective.

Black-eyed Susans Along the Barn
by Natalie Sewell (44" x 29")

This simple scene posed some complex challenges. Inspired by a photograph of Alaine Johnson's (see page 11), I was thrilled when I found the barn fabric in my stash since I had thought that creating wood would be the hard part.

What I didn't notice in the photo, until I had begun the design, was the hardware on the barn door. Little and inconspicuous, it proved to be the biggest challenge. How could I make fabric look like old rusty metal? I found a small piece of metallic-painted Skydye fabric (see Resource Page 142). But it didn't reflect light like metal did. I finally resorted to dabs of white pastel on the metallic fabric. The results are mixed.

The shadow on the slide lock is a strip of black fabric. So is the crack in the door.

The flowers are cut-up strips of a yellow hand-dyed fabric for the petals, and a black and spotted gold fabric that I found in my stash. Cut into little ovals, this amazingly ugly black fabric worked perfectly. To create depth, I colored the more distant petals dark orange so they looked as if they were shaded on the inside of the flower.

Lussier's Bridge by Natalie Sewell (41" x 35")

This quilt was inspired by a lovely bridge at Madison's Olbrich Botanical Gardens. I was hanging a show there and wanted to create a few scenes from the gardens themselves. It's been a few years since I created this quilt and I'd like to think my sense of perspective has improved since then. Nevertheless, the quilt belongs in this chapter on structure, because the bridge offered significant challenges.

Notice the bridge in the inspirational photo. The actual bridge swings slightly to the back of the scene. Not willing or able to tackle that depth yet, I treated it as if it ran parallel to the foreground, a technique I highly recommend to beginning landscape quilters. Note also the large dark shadow under the bridge in the inspirational photo. Because I had changed the perspective of the bridge, I also had to change the shadow. My solution was to show only the underside of the bridge in shade, as if I were standing lower in the scene than I actually was.

Notice in the above close-up photo, which depicts an early stage of the design, how flat the scene looks without shading or reflections. I added dark edges and spots on the foliage as well as structures to give the scene depth.

I took great liberties with the foliage by using fabrics with just texture rather than actual leaves. The key to depicting nature in landscape quilts is the same as it is in all art—always simplify.

Garden Gate
by Natalie Sewell and Nancy Zieman
(60" x 63")

Garden Gate was a joint effort that posed huge challenges. First, its mere size was daunting. We decided that a large canvas would allow room for both of us to work physically side by side. But we got carried away. Covering that much fabric with foliage proved difficult.

Secondly, we wanted the challenge of working with the perspective that the scene offered. Our inspiration was a watercolor greeting card set in a southern California beach town. We knew immediately that our Midwestern heads would change all the foliage and trees to look as if they grew in Wisconsin. But the three-dimensional perspective required to construct the steps and the gate was difficult, and though we came close, we didn't quite make it. Nevertheless, we learned plenty from making this quilt and are happy to share our process with you.

These are the foliage fabrics we chose for *Garden Gate*.

We started with the background fabric, a mottled yellow hand-dye for the upper portion, and a green and tan mottled print for the bottom. Then we positioned the large tree on the left. An upholstery fabric with blue and turquoise blotches for the tree trunk lifted our spirits almost as much as the expanse of green blobs on the bottom half of the scene dampened them. This is the hardest part of landscape quilting—getting past the ugliness of the first few stages.

We added two more hand-dyes to the foreground. Natalie began to work on the distant trees and ground cover while Nancy tackled the gate.

Natalie added lots of distant foliage while Nancy worked on bricks. We had very little "brick" fabric—the lines we drew on it had to be right the first time. They almost were.

We auditioned half a dozen flowers for the sides of the brick walk. Most were either too bland or too bright. Finally we found some pale purple irises that were the right scale but the wrong color. Yellow fabric markers solved that problem.

Wonderful as our upholstery fabric was for the trees, it wasn't quite detailed enough as our scene took shape. It often happens that as a scene nears completion, we see a need for added texture throughout the landscape, and especially in the foreground. We added mottled brown fabric and ran black fabric markers up and down the trunks to create more realistic texture.

Abandoned
by Natalie Sewell and Nancy Zieman
(63" x 54")

Not having learned our lesson about size with *Garden Gate*, we proceeded to make another huge quilt together. *Abandoned* was inspired by a photo in a garden book that featured a well-tended house and fence. The bedraggled look was our contribution—both because it was more interesting and because "bedraggled" and "neglected" are easier than well-tended.

Since a field of flowers is always nine-tenths leaves, our first job was to find a variety of scales of leaves, from middle-sized to small, with a variety of hues, from light to dark. These leaves formed the foundation of the field and guided our flower choices.

When we needed large, full flowers, we simply cut out what pieces we could find and glued them together. That was especially true for the ones that poked through the fence in the foreground. When we needed tiny ones, we cut them apart. Notice the sunflowers in front of the window in the photo below. Nancy found them in her dinner napkins while clearing the table one night and cut them up.

Then we chose flower fabrics, again with a variety of hues and sizes.

Because the structure in this scene is so clearly defined, the design came together quite quickly. Nancy worked on the shed, while Natalie worked on the distant tree. Then we both worked on the fence, leaving the field of flowers in the middle ground until the last.

This close-up shows you how the meadow began to come together. Notice how few flowers there are in the scene compared to leaves, and notice as well the dark spots in the foliage. The dark blotches are shadows of uneven foliage and places where the ground peeks through. Without them, the meadow looks artificial.

Notice the nail holes and the shading between the pickets

The Courtyard
By Natalie Sewell and Nancy Zieman
(38" x 36")

The Courtyard is another quilt that we designed together. But this time we had learned our lesson about size. A 38" by 36" quilt was easier to make even if we got in each other's way a bit during the design process.

We came to our quilting session prepared. We each had copies of the inspirational photo (from a gardening design book). Based on the photo, we decided that Nancy would work on the wall and flowering vines ahead of time, and Natalie would create the inner courtyard scene of grass and trees. That plan worked beautifully.

But trouble lay ahead. The photo depicted a stone walk that began in the foreground and went straight to the back of the scene. Had we been more experienced, we could have created a curved path and ignored our photo. But we weren't, as you can see in the photo to the right. When a family member wondered if we were creating a wedding scene because the path looked like a bridal veil we ripped it off and left the grass.

The gates also caused trouble. They were very ornate in the inspirational photo, so we simplified them. We tried drawing the bars in with black markers. But the lines weren't bold enough. So Nancy laboriously cut many tiny strips of black fabric for the bars. It took hours. Fortunately for us, that gate will never close so we won't have to find out if the two halves would truly meet in the middle.

Gazebo by Nancy Zieman (29" by 39")

One summer afternoon, after taping an episode of *Sewing With Nancy*, my TV staff and I made an uncharacteristic stop at Olbrich Botanical Gardens. We followed the designated paths through the beautifully designed gardens. When the path made a sharp right turn, we all made a collective gasp of wonder. What faced us was a gazebo in full bloom. It was a sight to capture on film and eventually on fabric.

Often Natalie and I will leave the photograph behind after gleaning several design elements from it. Not so this time. I studied and studied the structural elements, using fabric and marking pens instead of wood and nails to recreate the gazebo shape.

Notice in the photo that the gazebo roof is actually white, not brown. I initially tried a white roof but it was so bright it jumped off the canvas. After auditioning many "roof" fabrics, I finally settled for a mottled brown that looks like tin.

This small quilt, with its challenging structure, was hands down the most difficult quilt I've ever made!

Chapter 5
Creating Water Scenes

Fabric lends itself beautifully to water scenes. Add some fabric paint and horizontal quilting stitches and very realistic water scenes can come to life quickly and easily.

The most important component is your fabric. Hand-dyes are always our first choice for water for one simple reason—they have no repeats. An expanse of water is just that—water. Since you can't use foliage or flowers to cover up the repeated motifs that are the hallmark of commercial fabric, you have no way to hide them.

Another important reason for choosing hand-dyes for water is that they are gorgeous. Since water may well cover a large portion of your landscape scene, you do want to choose a beautiful fabric. Look for multi-hued tones with plenty of light and dark sections. Some even have horizontal markings that look like waves or currents. We save our favorite hand-dyed fabric purchases for future water scenes.

Water fabric does not have to be blue. Gray, yellow, green, purple, and sometimes all of these in the same fabric, make lovely water scenes. Your water fabric can also serve as the sky in your scene. All you need is a horizon line, which you can add easily with paint or a strip of fabric.

Red Canoe
by Natalie Sewell (45" x 41")

The Red Canoe by Natalie Sewell (45" x 41")

The Red Canoe started as a wooded scene and evolved into a water scene. (See page 10 in chapter one.) Because the water serves as the foreground, I drew dark horizontal lines on it here and there to define the scale. By separating the lines a bit, I created the sense of a close-up view.

The canoe was a challenge. I tried red batiks but they all blended into the surrounding nature scene. I had to resort to a bright red solid fabric to convey the man-made boat. I drew the canoe free-hand, but later realized that I could have enlarged my inspirational photo on a copy machine and created a template of the canoe. Although I loved the boat I realized that once the piece was quilted it would rumple just like the rest of the natural objects in the scene. To keep it smooth, I stuffed it with thin batting and a piece of fusible web.

Then, sucking up my courage, I tackled the reflection. Knowing that a red fabric paint or marker would never show on the dark blue water, I rubbed the area where the reflection would go with a white-out pen called Quick Fix, then covered the area with dark red fabric paint. It worked. A white pastel would have done just as well. When it came time to machine quilt the piece, I used horizontal lines of metallic thread here and there in the water to add sheen to the foreground.

The Yellow Canoe by Natalie Sewell (49" x 44")

I'm embarrassed to say that I was so happy with my red canoe that I made another one, this time yellow. Afraid to press my luck with the reflection, however, this time I beached the canoe. What drove me to repeat the canoe was how much I like the contrast between man-made elements and the lacy and multi-hued woods, grasses and lake. This concept of humans imposing their belongings on nature has also driven me to create clotheslines in the woods and rural mailboxes.

The water in this scene is in the distance. As it extends to the horizon it fades in intensity. I darkened the horizon line with a blue pastel and lightened the distant water with white. By waiting until the piece was quilted, I got some nice ripples as the pastel crayon ran over the quilting stitches.

The lacy woods are a stark contrast to the bright, solid canoe.

The Oregon Coast
by Natalie Sewell (40" by 29")

This cold, windy scene was inspired by a newspaper photo of the Pacific coast near Portland. I must confess I've never been to Portland and I've never seen a tree like the one depicted here. But as soon as I saw the photo, I thought, "Wow, I just bought all those fabrics and I can make this scene!" In the process of making the quilt, however, I became so fond of the tree, the rocks, and the shoreline that I resolved to get to Portland soon.

As you can see, most of the fabrics in the scene are Skydye hand-dyes, except for the grasses and the orange and gray batik. These Sky-dye's (see Resources, page 142) were made with pearlescent ink, which casts a metallic shine—a very effective glimmer for water and rocks.

The background fabric serves as both water and sky. After I added the jagged, dark gray rocks, I dotted the water around them with a white pastel to create the image of waves crashing on them.

The orange foreground is cut from the batik. I covered much of it with messy-cut grass fabric and allowed only a peek at the sun-dappled ground. The tree trunk is a strip of brown batik—the branches and leaves are painted on. The border is an ombré fabric that fades from brown to champagne, and lends itself well to having grasses extend over it to the bottom of the quilt.

In this early stage of my scene the hand-dyed fabric is doing most of the work.

When I added the purple mountain range which separates the sky from the water, I allowed the hand-dyed fabric's markings to remain as distant mountains covered with low-hanging clouds.

The Boat Dock *by Nancy Zieman (45" x 30")*

One of the many pleasures of landscape quilting is the chance it offers to present a special gift to a family member. My daughter-in-law, Alison, admired this quilt as I was working on it. She said it reminded her of her childhood, growing up near the Mississippi River. The quilt now hangs in her living room.

For the foliage fabrics, I used many shades of green with light and dark highlights, and a variety of scales.

As in all the landscape quilts featured in this chapter, the background fabric is the most critical. This background fabric has a sateen finish which adds to the luster of the water.

When I began working on *The Boat Dock*, I thought I was going to make a wooded scene. But after I cut and glued the distant trees, and then stood back to look at my work, I saw water in the foreground. I then abandoned my plans and let the fabric have its way.

Now that my woods had become a water scene, it needed a focal point. A boat dock seemed to be the perfect solution. After a little research, I found a photo of a dock to use as a model.

I used the same fabric markers for adding reflections in the water as I used for shading the trees. Since I didn't want dark reflections, I tested the pens first on a scrap. The ones that were almost dried out worked the best for creating reflections.

Peaceful *by Nancy Zieman (44" x 30")*

A trip to Rocky Mountain National Park was the inspiration for this landscape design. A foreground of aspen trees with mountains in the background and a lake in the middle made for a tranquil scene.

Initially, I extended only the largest of trees into the borders. Thinking I was finished, I hung the quilt in our family room. Two weeks later, I took the quilt down from the wall and added extensions to two more trees. I often find myself adding elements to a design after I think it's finished.

This photo shows an early version of the quilt. I wasn't happy with the design at that point. Cropping the mountains and reducing the size of the water greatly improved the final product.

Evening at the Pond
by Natalie Sewell and Nancy Zieman (57" x 45")

Inspired by a gorgeous photograph in a nature book, *Evening at the Pond* is really a "whole cloth" quilt. That is, except for the relatively few trees and foliage, the sky and water are all one piece of fabric. We had purchased it in Paducah at the American Quilter's Society show a few years ago and knew at the time that we would be saving this large piece of hand-dyed fabric for a special joint quilt. Together, we leafed through dozens of inspirational photos until we found one that would allow us to keep much of the hand-dyed fabric exposed.

The wide range of hues in the hand-dye—mauve, blue, purple, green—were too dark for a daytime scene so we assigned it to evening. We painted in many of the distant trees, the trees reflected in the water, and the shadows at the shoreline. The scene is a distant one, so all the foliage fabrics have small scale dot patterns rather than individual leaves. We used a wide variety of ground cover fabrics.

The border is also a hand-dyed fabric. We chose it because it echoed the dappled light of the water itself. This quilt confirms one of our pet theories: Don't interrupt when a piece of fabric is trying to tell you something. Let your fabric work for you.

Notice the difference between the finished quilt and this photo. The lack of shading makes this stage of the design look flat.

As you can see in this close-up photo of the finished quilt, the water is quilted horizontally and the sky is stippled—and that is the only difference between them. (See Chapter Seven for stippling directions, page 137.)

Summer Morning *by Nancy Zieman (28" x 30")*

Summer Morning is a very simple quilt, an ideal beginner's scene, especially if you use a hand-dyed fabric for your background and an interesting batik for the border.

I created a horizon line one-third of the way down from the top of the background fabric to divide the sky from the water. When you break up a scene this way, keep in mind the basic principle of thirds for design proportions. If you glance over to the next page, you'll see that Natalie used the same proportions in her quilt, *Jasmine Arbor*.

I'm always amazed to find that a few details, such as rocks, can add interesting details.

Jasmine Arbor by Natalie Sewell (40" x 42")

Jasmine Arbor is another easy horizon line quilt. This time, however, the horizon line is a range of multi-hued mountains and foothills. The water and sky are again one piece of fabric. For the first two years of this quilt's life, it looked like the photo below, an expanse of water surrounded by a jasmine vine on an arbor. One day I added a sailboat. The jury's is still out on whether the boat will remain.

I love to hand-appliqué but rarely get the chance. So whenever I can, I hand-make bias trim from hand-dyed fabrics for arbors and vines on my landscapes and sew it on by hand.

Lookout Point
by Natalie Sewell and Nancy Zieman (55" x 36")

A snapshot taken on Washington Island in Door County, Wisconsin became the inspiration for this scene. Because the photo was taken at sunset when the sky was truly coral, we were lucky to find a gorgeous Skydye with the same coral and blue hues. Having matched the sky and water so perfectly, we stayed very close to the photo for the rest of the scene as well.

The horizon line is thick gray marker and the ripples in the water are part hand-dyed marks and part gray pastel. We exaggerated the markings in the fabric that we liked. Notice also that the water is quilted with horizontal lines and the sky is stippled to help the viewer differentiate between them.

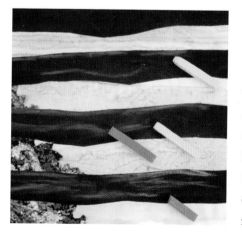

This photo shows the pastels we used to shade the fence. Given that the time of day we're depicting is sunset, we used coral, pink, yellow and turquoise to illuminate the light hitting the rails. Because it worked so well we made a mental note to add a variety of colors to sun-kissed light spots in future quilts.

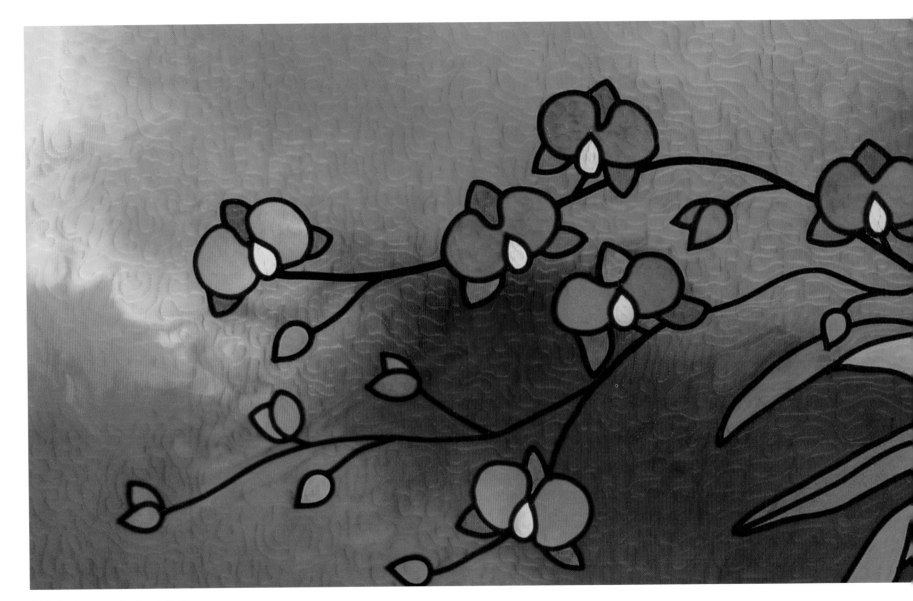

Chapter 6
Creating Stylized Quilts

Not all landscape quilts need to have realistic colors. In this chapter we feature some of our more stylized quilts. Some are made with silk fabric in brilliant colors, others are fashioned after stained glass, one is a challenge quilt with wild and crazy fabric requirements. Yet all are made with the same techniques we use for more natural landscape scenes. We include them here to show you the many options that scissors, glue and raw-edged appliqué offer for artistic interpretation. The design possibilities are endless.

Silk Orchids
by Nancy Zieman (41" x 21")

Spiderwort by Nancy Zieman
(31" x 27")

Many people who see this landscape quilt comment on my "orchid" design. In truth, it's not an orchid at all, but a spiderwort, inspired by a plant my neighbor found along a railroad track and kindly gave to me.

The periwinkle blooms of the spiderwort plant make a wonderful contrast to its chartreuse foliage.

I used only four fabrics in this design. The hand-dyed green fabric was the ideal choice for the leaves. I cut the stamen from the print and the blooms from the purple batik. The busy background fabric is not one I would ordinarily recommend. However, it works well in this stylized design.

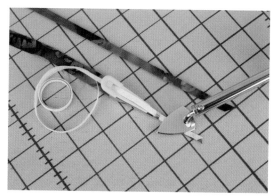

I used pastels to shade the leaves and the blossoms. I simply "colored" within the lines of the cutout leaves and petals. Experiment with this technique. If you don't like the first result, cut another set of leaves and blooms and try again. It's a great way to learn the process.

Rather than bordering the quilt, I added narrow strips of trim. Using a ¼" fusible bias tape maker, I cut half inch strips of fabric, inserted them through the wide end of the maker (notice that fusible strips of web were inserted through this notion), advanced the strips to the narrow end with a pin, and pressed. Before positioning the trim on the quilt, I removed the paper backing from the trim. The fusible temporarily holds the trim in place when pressed. Later, I stitched the trim to the background fabric.

Day Lily Garden *by Nancy Zieman*
(45" x 32")

At heart, I'm a gardener. During winter months I "garden" with fabric. During the rest of the year I garden with the real things—plants and soil. Dirt under my fingernails refreshes my soul.

Unlike my outside garden, my *Day Lily Garden* landscape design is blooming with pink blossoms. My real garden features orange day lilies. I secretly wish my real lilies were pink. So, pink they are in this impressionistic design.

I couldn't find a flower print of day lilies so I improvised once again. The orchid designs in this fabric had many of the characteristics of a day lily whose petals have pointed ends. Creative cutting made it happen.

Tulips In Bloom *by Natalie Sewell (40" x 31")*

I made this impressionistic flower quilt for a flower challenge at a national quilt show. I had created a similar design before—using a navy hand-dyed fabric for the background and simply leaving the fore-ground and distance up to the viewer's imagination. But this time, armed with my new tool, pastels, I swiped each tulip blossom with a white pastel. The effect was one of sunlight hitting the flowers. This simple trick brought the scene to life.

Wisteria
by Natalie Sewell (40" x 31")

I love doing hand-appliqué and had so enjoyed making a stained-glass wisteria scene a few years ago that I decided to make another one. I made my own bias trim for the arbor and the vines, and lightly glued the backs of each bias bar so I could press them into place on the background fabric.

As each vine approached a bar of the arbor, I lifted it so I could twist the vine around and under it. The wisteria blossoms are messy cut from a blue batik and the leaves from a variety of hand-dyed green fabrics. After the leaves, vines and blossoms were in place on the background fabric, I outlined each of them with fabric markers.

After machine quilting the piece, I spent weeks and weeks happily hand appliquéing all the bars and vines. Any quilt with that much handwork in it had to be given to a friend. I gave it to Nancy.

Tiffany Grapes *by Natalie Sewell*
(21" by 42")

"Stained glass" quilts are easy to design and fun to make. No realistic scenery means no three dimensional images—just repeated motifs arranged attractively. These scenes are great for beginners or anyone who wants to become comfortable with the technique before launching an ambitious landscape.

What makes the quilt look like stained glass are the hand-dyed fabrics and the outlining of the motifs with fabric paint or markers. Buying ready made bias trim for the vines makes the project easy as well as attractive.

Clematis *by Natalie Sewell*
(18" x 42")

This little quilt features a hand-dyed background fabric and some colorful blooms from a print. It can be designed quickly, and, if made without a border, quilted and bound in no time. It makes a lovely small wall hanging or table runner.

Oriental Fantasy by Natalie Sewell
(35" x 38")

In response to an invitational challenge sponsored by Pilgrim/Roy a few years ago, I agreed to make a quilt. But when the fabrics I was required to use came in the mail, I almost changed my mind. As you can see in the below photo, they are the least likely landscape fabrics one could imagine. The collection also included a black fabric (not pictured).

I studied these unpromising fabrics carefully and, with the inspiration of a Japanese greeting card as my guide, created the design. I took advantage of the two leaf prints for the foliage in the tree and on the ground. The variegated chartreuse provided some nice grass, and the bright yellow some brilliant sky. But it was still a garish scene.

The only embellishment I was allowed to use was embroidery thread. So I embroidered heavily. First I tested the embroidery threads on a scrap of background fabric. Because this was a challenge and I had a limited fabric supply I couldn't take chances.

As you can see in the photo to the right, I used silver metallic embroidery thread to create a gnarled trunk. I used pink and blue thread to add texture to the leaves and ground cover.

If there's a message this quilt bestowed on me, it certainly was "accept all challenges." In the process of tackling this quilt, I learned how to turn just about any fabric into a landscape quilt.

Silk Orchids *by Nancy Zieman (41" x 21")*

A few years ago at a quilt show I purchased two pieces of multi-hued hand-dyed silk. Both pieces were similar in color. It was one of those impulse purchases, as I didn't have a clue how I was going to use them.

After receiving an orchid plant as a gift, I knew the two fabrics were destined to become an orchid design. I used one piece for the background, and the other for the leaves and blooms. I added bias trim to give the quilt a stained-glass appearance.

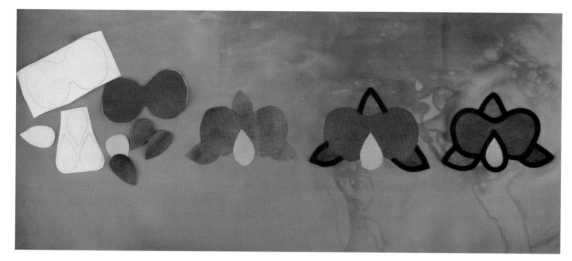

Because the fabrics were slippery, I used a paper-backed fusible web (HeatnBond Lite) rather than a glue stick to position the silk elements on the silk background.

Notice that the trim on the stems is wider than the trim covering the blossoms. I used ¼" bias trim for the heavier stems and stitched it down by machine along each side after I added the batting and backing fabrics.

Using a mini-iron was helpful for working with the small details.

The photo above shows my progression for creating the orchid. First I traced the design elements on the paper side of the web. Then I fused the web to the wrong side of the silk and cut out the shapes. Next I fused the shapes to the background, and then used ⅛" bias trim to cover the edges. Finally I fused the trim to the background elements and then covered the foreground edges.

Mary's Orchids by Nancy Zieman
(24" x 26")

Once I design a quilt I like, I tend to make more of the same. After I finished *Silk Orchids* I was eager to use another hand-dyed silk in a scene. *Mary's Orchids* is similar to *Silk Orchids* but without the bias trim.

I used only one length of a hand-dyed silk for both the background and design elements. I cut off one end of the silk that had both warm and cool tones and used it for the leaves and petal fabric. Before cutting, I took time to fold under the portion of the silk panel that I thought I would cut off, pinned it to my design wall, and studied the size. I was nervous that I would cut off too much fabric. As the Russian proverb states, "Measure three times, cut once."

The quilt now hangs in my friend, Mary Mulari's, home.

Irises On Silk by Nancy Zieman
(23" x 27")

Natalie was with me the day that I purchased several panels of silk hand-dyed fabric. Since our landscape minds think alike, she made a purchase as well. After I showed her the finished version of *Mary's Orchids*, Natalie handed over her silk hand-dyed fabric to me and said, "This fabric is too bright for me. It's more your style."

I eventually returned the fabric to Natalie as a finished landscape quilt. I used batik fabrics for the leaves and an iris print for the blossoms. Unlike my other two silk pieces, this one combines silk and cotton fabrics.

Chapter 7
Finishing Touches

Once you've finished designing your landscape quilt top, you're ready to turn it into a wall hanging. Here's where craftsmanship counts.

Designing the scene is a spontaneous process with very few rules. Not so for the finishing techniques. The craft of quilting is intricate and precise. It requires you to obey many rules. What follows are some general guidelines for completing your scene, including sewing down your quilt top, squaring it up, adding borders, machine quilting, and binding. We also share tips for making a hanging sleeve and labeling your quilt.

Here's a cautionary note to beginners. The guidelines in this chapter cannot substitute for a thorough quilting class or book that describes in full detail how to construct a quilt. If you are new to quilting we recommend that you sign up for a beginner's class or buy a book for beginning quilting techniques or both. The guidelines in this chapter are meant only as reminders and tips.

Lake Huron
by Natalie Sewell (39" x 37")

The quilt depicted on these pages is *Lake Huron* by Natalie Sewell, who did indeed finish the quilt as we wrote the book so each step could be photographed and described.

Machine-Stitch the Quilt Top

Gluing the fabric pieces to the background fabric temporarily holds the design together. Once you're satisfied with your scene, you are ready to machine stitch the glued pieces to the background fabric. This step will keep all the sections permanently in place.

Set Up Your Sewing Machine

1. Lower the feed dogs. Check your owner's manual if you are unsure of how to make this adjustment.
2. Reduce the upper tension by two numbers or notches.
3. Insert a size 70, 75 or 80 needle, either a Universal, Sharp or Quilting. The Universal is a good overall quilting needle; however, it leaves a larger hole in the fabric. The Sharp makes a smaller hole, but tends to break more easily. For beginners, the Quilting #75 leaves a small hole but is strong enough for inexperienced quilters. Check your owner's manual if you are unsure how to change the needle in your sewing machine.
4. Thread the needle with nylon monofilament thread. The clear thread blends in with any fabric, eliminating the need to change thread colors as you go. It also allows you to double stitch over a line of quilting several times without it showing. This is an important advantage when you are working with raw-edge designs.
5. Match the bobbin thread to the background color. If you can't decide among several colors, choose the one that's slightly darker than your background fabric.
6. Attach a darning foot and adjust the machine for a straight stitch.

Stitch Around the Edges

1. Use rubber fingers available from office supply stores to control the fabric.
2. Lower the presser foot to the darning or sewing position. The foot will glide slightly above the fabric.
3. Place your hands evenly on both sides of the needle, gently holding the quilt top in place.
4. Guide the fabric with your hands. Since the feed dogs are lowered, you—not the machine—will control the fabric.
5. Move the fabric at an even speed and stitch along the edges of each motif just enough to anchor the pieces in place. If you stitch close to the cut edges with small enough stitches, you will not have to remove this stitching later on.

Press the Quilt Top

After stitching the motifs in place, press the entire quilt top on the wrong side with a steam iron. If puckers appear, break the thread with your seam ripper and flatten the area with more steam. You probably won't have to re-stitch this section as other stitches will hold it into place until you layer the piece.

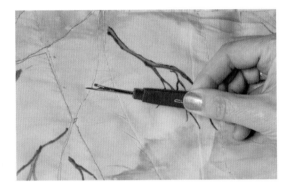

Square Up the Quilt Top

It's important to make sure your quilt top is a perfect rectangle before you add borders. Otherwise your quilt will not hang flat on the wall. Take all the time you need to do this step carefully. We've been known to spend hours making sure that the corners are perfect right angles and the opposite sides of the quilt top are the same length.

1. Fold the quilt top in half and place it on a cutting mat. Align the fold with one of the marked lines on the mat. Using a ruler and a rotary cutter, trim the right and left edges, cutting parallel to the fold.

2. Unfold the quilt top and refold it in the opposite direction, meeting side edges. Trim side edges, again cutting parallel to the fold with a rotary cutter and ruler.

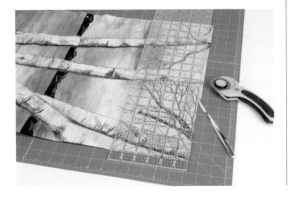

3. Unfold the quilt top and use a large square ruler to check that each corner is a 90-degree angle. If necessary, repeat the folding and trimming process until all the corners are perfect 90-degree angles.

4. Pin the quilt top to your design wall and check the size of each side of your quilt by measuring from the top to the bottom, from left to right, and from corner to corner.

5. Steam the quilt top with your iron, pressing from the wrong side, to flatten and stabilize it. Let the quilt top dry.

Add the Borders

A landscape quilt's border serves the same purpose as the frame of a painting—
it directs attention to the scene. Because landscape quilts can be very busy, a good border
surrounds the scene with peace and quiet at the same time that it highlights the focal point.

Audition Border Choices

Landscape quilts can be busy scenes. The best way to choose the color and size of your border is to audition a variety of fabrics. With your quilt top pinned on your design wall, try out several choices in several widths to find the one that works best.

We find that choosing borders is one of the most difficult aspects of landscape quilting. To make the decision easier we often send each other digital photos of our designs with a variety of fabrics pinned along the sides as border choices.

We highly recommend asking friends or family members to help you decide which fabric to choose. At least give yourself time to consider border options under different lights at different times of the day. A border choice made at night under artificial light may look quite different in the light of day. Another option is to simply bind the quilt.

Natalie auditioned both of these border fabrics before choosing the one on the left, for her quilt, Lake Huron.

Cut the Borders

Cut four outer border lengths: two borders 8" longer than the sides and two borders 8" longer than the top and bottom edges. Common border widths range from 2" to 4" depending on the size of your scene.

If you have enough yardage, cut your border strips from the length of the fabric—parallel to the selvage. The length is much more stable than the selvage and has no stretch to it. Therefore, your borders will lie flatter against the wall when you hang your quilt.

To add an inner border, cut 1"-wide pieces the same lengths as your outer borders. Stitch the inner borders to the outer borders with a ¼" seam allowance. Press the seams toward the outer border.

Miter the Borders

1. Pin and sew a border to each side of the quilt, making certain that 4" of the border extends at each end. Sew with ¼" seam allowances. Stop sewing ¼" from each corner.

2. Smooth one of the corner borders flat. Fold the adjoining border, aligning the outer edges of the two-border strips to create a 45-degree mitered corner.

3. Press along the fold.

4. Pin the borders together at the mitered edge.

5. Fold back the quilt top, exposing the wrong side and the press mark.

6. Stitch along the press mark, sewing to the point of the miter. Trim the seam allowance to ¼".

7. Press open the seam allowance. Repeat steps 1 through 6 at each corner.

Layer Your Quilt

1. Choose a backing fabric that is at least 2" to 3" larger than your bordered quilt top. We like to select backing fabrics that fit the mood of our landscape scene. For the backing of *Lake Huron* Natalie chose a blue and gray mottled print fabric.

2. Place the backing wrong side up on a flat surface, such as a table or the floor. Secure the backing to the surface with masking tape. Give the corners a little tug, stretching them gently so that the backing is completely smooth. This helps eliminate puckers as you machine-quilt.

3. Use a lightweight batting; "Warm and Natural" by the Warm Company is Natalie's favorite. Place the batting on top of the backing and smooth it out with your hands. Then place the quilt top right side up on the batting.

4. Pin the layers of the quilt together with safety pins or curved basting pins. Space pins about 3" apart, or no further apart than the size of your fist. This adequately secures the layers, yet won't interfere with the machine quilting process.

Free-Motion Quilt Your Scene

Free-motion quilting will secure the three layers of your quilt together. This stitching is what gives your quilt its texture and personality. Once you gain experience free-motion quilting, you will find it as enjoyable and relaxing as we do.

When we free-motion quilt our landscape scenes, we are always doing one of two things. We are either outlining the motifs we find in the fabric or stippling.

Outline stitching is simply tracing the fabric elements as we sew. When we see leaves, we stitch their outlines and perhaps a vein or two. When we come to flowers, we stitch along the petal lines and make little circles in the stamen. We follow the lines of the tree trunks up and down, not quilting at all on the bark unless the tree is more than 3" or 4" wide. We stitch along either side of branches and make jagged stitches in grass. In short, we let the fabric suggest the stitch pattern.

Here Natalie has stippled the sky and outline stitched the tree trunks.

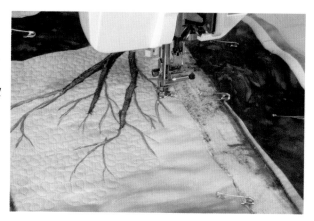

When we stitch an area of our scene that has no significant printed pattern, such as sky, water, or distant ground cover and foliage, we stipple. Stippling is the process of filling spaces in the quilt scene or border with small stitches in tiny, curvy lines usually no bigger than ¼" apart. Each quilter develops her own unique style of stippling. Nancy makes leaf shapes; Natalie makes puzzle pieces. Once you become proficient at stippling you will have your own stippling "signature."

Becoming comfortable with stippling does take practice and experience. Because landscape scenes are often busy, they make ideal "practice grounds." No-one will notice if your curves cross over each other now and then, or a few stitches here and there are a little too big.

Guidelines for Free-motion Quilting

Whether you are outline stitching or stippling, the following guidelines for free-motion quilting apply.

1. Lower the feed dogs, thread the needle with monofilament thread and attach a darning foot.
2. Begin stitching at the center and work out to the borders. If your quilt is much larger than your work table, roll the quilt toward the center from each end. Complete the entire landscape scene before you begin to machine quilt the borders.
3. Remove the safety pins one by one as you come to them. The ones remaining will help to keep the fabric layers from shifting while you sew.

4. Stitch with the same intensity throughout the quilt and the borders. If you've stitched heavily and finely in the center of the quilt, do the same in the rest of the scene and in the borders. If your quilt is unevenly stitched, it will not lie flat. If your border is not stitched as heavily as the rest of the scene, it will pucker.

Stipple the Borders

Once you've completed quilting your scene, raise your feed dogs and with a quilting foot engaged, stitch a line in the ditch between your scene and the border. We often add a second line ½" into the border which creates a mat around your scene. This touch adds stability to your wall hanging and helps to ensure that it will lie flat.

Now you're ready to drop your feed dogs again and stipple the rest of the border.

Bind Your Quilt

Binding adds a finishing touch to the edges of your quilt. Follow these instructions to make a ½" double-fold French binding.

1. Cut straight-grain binding strips 3" wide. Join the strips as needed to have sufficient length for all four sides of the quilt. Joining strips on the bias (by joining with a diagonal seam) reduces bulk when the binding is folded to the wrong side.

2. Cut the end of the strip at a 45-degree angle. Fold in ¼" at one short end of the binding. (Optional: Press a ¼" strip of paper-backed fusible web on top of the folded-under edge.) Fold the binding in half, with wrong sides together, meeting lengthwise edges and press.

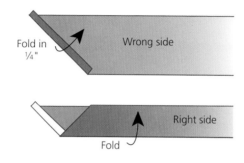

3. Mark the quilt top ¼" from each corner.

Mark ¼" from corners

4. Meet cut edges of the binding to the quilt top, beginning at the center of one edge of the quilt, with right sides together. Stitch the binding to the quilt top with a ¼" seam, stopping stitching at the marked point. Lock stitches by stitching in place or stitch in reverse.

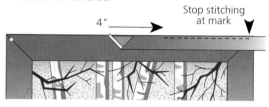

5. Fold the binding up at a 45-degree angle, aligning the cut edges of the binding with the cut edge of the quilt.

6. Fold the binding down, meeting the binding fold to the top edge of the quilt and the binding cut edges to the quilt side edges. Stitch a ¼" seam on the side, starting at the marked point. Repeat at the remaining corners.

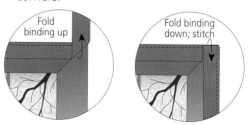

7. When the binding reaches the starting point again overlap the binding and trim the excess. (If a strip of paper-backed fusible web was used, remove the paper backing from the folded-under end of the binding.)

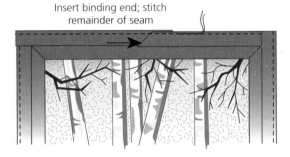

Insert binding end; stitch remainder of seam

8. Fold and press the binding away from the quilt.
9. Fold the binding to the wrong side, covering the stitch line and tucking in the corners to form miters. Hand-stitch the folded edges of the binding to the quilt backing.

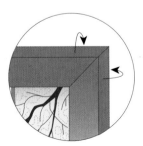

Add a Quilt Sleeve

A quilt sleeve lets you display your quilt on a wall after it has been completed. The sleeve described below doesn't pinch the corners and becomes invisible on the wall.

1. Cut an 8" strip of fabric from the backing fabric, cutting the strip 1" shorter than the width of the quilt. Turn under ¼" at both short ends of the strip and press.
2. Fold the strip in half, with right sides together, meeting the lengthwise edges. Stitch a ¼" seam along the lengthwise edge to form a tube. Turn the tube right-side out and press.
3. Center the tube on the upper edge of the quilt, positioning it ½" from the top. Hand-stitch along the lower fold. Fold back the sleeve ½" from the top fold; pin the ½" tuck the length of the sleeve. Hand-stitch the sleeve to the quilt, catching only the first layer of the fabric. The recessed stitching allows the quilt to hang parallel to the wall without buckling or pulling down the corners.

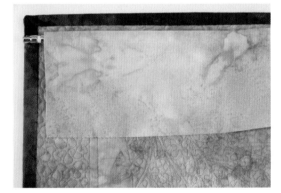

Trim Loose Threads and Edges

Give your finished landscape quilt a "haircut" to remove any edges of fabric that have become fringed, fuzzy or whiskered. Machine appliquéing inevitably leaves frayed edges and loose threads—now is the time to remove as many as you can. Place the quilt on your lap; using sharp embroidery scissors, hold the blades of the scissors parallel to the quilt top and trim stray threads and frayed fabric edges. After you've finished trimming the quilt top, turn the quilt over and clip any loose bobbin threads from the back.

Block Your Quilt

Blocking gives your quilt a finished look. No matter how careful your craftsmanship, inevitably a corner of your quilt will curl a little or a section will buckle. Blocking your quilt on a vertical surface with plenty of hot steam will convince it to lie flat against the wall.

1. Return you quilt to your design wall. Pin it in place and pin any section that buckles or curls.
2. Using a small damp towel, cover a section of the quilt. Press the quilt through the towel, using a hot iron. The process should provide plenty of steam.
3. Move the damp towel to the next area of the quilt. Re-wet the towel when necessary. Press.
4. Pin the bottom corners flat and make sure the quilt is hanging as it should. Allow the quilt to dry overnight on the vertical surface.

Label Your Quilt

Your finished quilt deserves a label. Here's a simple quick option that provides the needed information and maintains the mood you created in your landscape quilt.

1. Cut a rectangle, approximately 4" x 6", of light-colored fabric that coordinates with the backing fabric. Press under ¼" seam allowances along all sides.
2. Cut out and glue a few motifs that you used on the quilt front. Outline stitch around the motifs.
3. With a permanent marker, write your quilt's name, your name and the date you completed the quilt on the label.
4. Hand-stitch the label to a lower corner of your quilt's backing.

Resources

HAND-DYED FABRICS

Artfabrik
Laura Wasilowski
324 Vincent Place
Elgin, IL 60123
Phone: 847-931-7684
Web: www.artfabrik.com

Confetti Works
Sharon Luehring
The Stitcher's Crossing, Ltd.
6122 Mineral Point Road
Madison, WI 53705
Phone: 608-232-1500
E-mail: info@stitcherscrossing.com

Quilt Tapestry Studio
Wendy Richardson
8009 Florida Avenue North
Brooklyn Park, MN 55445
Phone: 763-566-3339
E-mail: wendyRQTS@aol.com

Skydyes
Mickey Lawler
P.O. Box 370116
West Hartford, CT 06137-0116
Phone: 860-232-1429
Web: www.skydyes.com

Annie's Attic
1 Annie Lane
Big Sandy, TX 75755
Phone: 800-582-6643
Web: www.anniesattic.com

Clotilde LLC
P.O. Box 7500
Big Sandy, TX 75755-7500
Phone: 800-772-2891
Web: www.clotilde.com

Connecting Threads
P.O. Box 870760
Vancouver, WA 98687-7760
Phone: 800-574-6454
Web: www.ConnectingThreads.com

Ghee's
2620 Centenary Blvd. No. 2-250
Shreveport, LA 71104
Phone: 318-226-1701
E-mail: bags@ghees.com
Web: www.ghees.com

Herrschners, Inc.
2800 Hoover Road
Stevens Point, WI 54492-0001
Phone: 800-441-0838
Web: www.herrschners.com

Home Sew
P.O. Box 4099
Bethlehem, PA 18018-0099
Phone: 800-344-4739
Web: www.homesew.com

Keepsake Quilting
Route 25
P.O. Box 1618
Center Harbor, NH 03226-1618
Phone: 800-438-5464
Web: www.keepsakequilting.com

Krause Publications
700 E. State Street
Iola WI, 54990
Phone: 888-457-4873
Web: www.krausebooks.com

Nancy's Notions
333 Beichl Ave.
P.O. Box 683
Beaver Dam, WI 53916-0683
Phone: 800-833-0690
Web: www.nancysnotions.com

Index

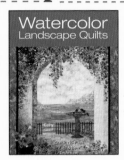